ARMS TRADE

Essential Issues

ARMS
TRADE

BY ASHLEY RAE HARRIS

Content Consultant
David Kinsella
Professor of Political Science and International Studies
Portland State University

ABDO
Publishing Company

CREDITS

Published by ABDO Publishing Company, 8000 West 78th Street, Edina, Minnesota 55439. Copyright © 2011 by Abdo Consulting Group, Inc. International copyrights reserved in all countries. No part of this book may be reproduced in any form without written permission from the publisher. The Essential Library™ is a trademark and logo of ABDO Publishing Company.

Printed in the United States of America,
North Mankato, Minnesota
112010
012011

 THIS BOOK CONTAINS AT LEAST 10% RECYCLED MATERIALS.

Editor: Jessica Hillstrom
Copy Editor: Paula Lewis
Interior Design and Production: Marie Tupy
Cover Design: Marie Tupy

Library of Congress Cataloging-in-Publication Data
Harris, Ashley Rae.
  Arms trade / by Ashley Rae Harris.
    p. cm. -- (Essential issues)
  Includes bibliographical references.
  ISBN 978-1-61714-770-8
  1. Arms transfers--Juvenile literature. 2. Defense industries--Juvenile literature. I. Title.
  HD9743.A2H374 2011
  382'.456234--dc22

                                    2010041183

TABLE OF CONTENTS

A young Somali boy with an AK-47 led fighters in military exercises in Mogadishu, January 1, 2010.

BORN TO KILL

Abdi lives in Somalia. He lives with his mother and sister in a hut with no running water or electricity. His father died from a bullet wound at age 19 when Abdi was just a baby. Abdi's brother was also shot and killed at 18. Abdi has never been to school. He spends his days hanging out with other boys and men on the dirt road near the gated barrier called the Mandera Triangle. The area is called a triangle because it is the meeting point of three African countries: Kenya, Ethiopia, and Somalia. Sometimes guards stand outside the gates. But for the most part, people can pass through from one country to another without being stopped by anyone.

During the day, Abdi and other teenage boys sit around watching girls and chewing on green leaves they call *khat*. Abdi likes khat because it makes him feel buzzed and excited. Plus, he does not feel as hungry when he chews it—there is rarely enough food to satisfy his growing teenage body.

Abdi carries a firearm with him at all times, just like all the other boys. His weapon is an AK-47 rifle that was left by the Russians almost 20 years ago. He got it by stealing food and tools to bring back to an older man named Erasto. Though the name means

Mandera Triangle

The Mandera Triangle is a major hub of illegal weapon trafficking in Africa. Weapons are easily smuggled between countries, and a significant amount of conflict exists between Kenya, Ethiopia, and Somalia. In many ways, corrupt governments and police have contributed to the violence. In October 2008, a Kenyan police-military operation raided ten towns and villages under the guise of disarming warring militias. In reality, they injured, raped, and killed civilians en masse while confiscating their weapons.

"peaceful man," Erasto is anything but peaceful. He is mean, but Abdi tries to stay on his good side. Abdi has seen Erasto shoot a man in the back.

At 15 years of age, this is the third firearm Abdi has carried with him. The others were stolen. He hopes that if people know he works for Erasto, they will not mess with him or steal from him anymore.

At night, Abdi and some of the others set up checkpoints, places where travelers must stop and be approved before continuing down their path. When people try to walk through a checkpoint, Abdi and the others stand guard with their weapons and demand that the people give them whatever money or goods they have with them. If those who are stopped are women, things can become very ugly. The boys may assault them to show their power. Abdi has watched as women and girls, just like his own mother and sister, have been raped and beaten.

Even though his mother wishes Abdi was not part of the violence, he remembers that she was happy

Khat

Though considered to be a drug of abuse by the World Health Organization and an illegal controlled substance in many countries, khat is legal to produce, buy, and sell in many regions. This leafy plant contains the stimulant cathinone, which causes euphoria and excitement, and can lead to dependency. The US Drug Enforcement Administration launched the Operation Somalia Express investigation in 2006 in an effort to track and dismantle the smuggling of khat from Africa to the United States.

when he got his first gun at age 12. Without it, there would be no way for him to protect his family or get any money to feed them. Even though no companies in Somalia make firearms, the weapons are easy to come by. It seems like every man in Abdi's village is either armed or dead.

With an AK-47 strapped around his torso, Abdi feels powerful. He can see the look of fear cross people's faces when they see him approach. Without it, he is just a skinny teenager. But with it, he is a killer.

BORN INTO WAR

In African countries, as well as in many other nations all over the world, children and adults just like Abdi were born into violence and poverty. Many later become violent killers. According to research done by the Small Arms Survey, the availability of small arms has increased violence and become a major problem. Robert Muggah, research director of the Small Arms Survey,

Violence against Women in Somalia

Women are pawns in violent civil wars. Terrorists and insurgents sometimes use rape or other forms of sexual abuse as a tool to spread fear and panic in a region. Sexual violence against women has become so commonplace in Somalia that women are raped in front of bystanders in the middle of the day. In war-torn Mogadishu, as many as 50 women seek help every month from relief agencies after being brutally raped. Many have learned to travel only to certain places and in groups. They must be especially fearful of passing through checkpoints. As one Somali woman says, "We're frightened of guns. . . . When we move, we have to go in groups."[1]

says that the availability of guns is "like an epidemic. In the same way the HIV/AIDS is an epidemic."[2]

There are at least 550 million known firearms around the world today. Governments, militaries, the United Nations (UN), and various organizations have made some effort to track and control the spread of weapons. However, there are tens to hundreds of millions of illegal or private firearms whose whereabouts are unknown.

Firearms are difficult to track for a number of reasons. They are small and easy to transport, so illegal trade is easy to hide from governing agencies. There is also a lack of laws that apply to arms trade

Killing Fields of Somalia

Somalia has very limited resources. When its dictator Mohammed Siad Barre was overthrown in 1991, the country was left without a central government. The people were desperate and different clans began to fight one another. For the past two decades, the country has been in a state of constant violence. Firearms have allowed insurgents and street militia to devastate entire villages in just days or hours. Men, women, and children are killed, cattle are raided, and homes are burned to the ground.

The only people benefiting from these violent circumstances are those who are involved in the gun trade. As one rebel says, "War drives the price of guns. Constant warfare is good for business."[3] In recent years, these killing fields have migrated into northern Kenya. Meanwhile, local organizers, many of them pastoralists, would like to repair the local economy through agricultural development. They believe they can begin to fix the problem only if they start at its root: gun manufacturers.

internationally. So brokers, or agents, can find ways to avoid the law yet still conduct unethical business. The issue is that small arms are traded to regions of the world that are unstable. Additional firearms only add to the problem.

The most deadly and most common are small arms or light weapons. Though they may seem less dangerous than a bomb, small arms are used more frequently and can be easily transported from one region to another. So their threat to a region's stability is larger.

Small Arms, Big Issue

Weapons are manufactured and distributed in many areas of the world. While Russia, Germany, France, and the United Kingdom are the source of many weapons, the United States is the largest exporter of firearms to the most dangerous and terrorist-ridden areas of the world. The United States produces more than half of the

What Are Small Arms and Light Weapons?

The United Nations defines small arms as:
• Revolvers and self-loading pistols
• Rifles and carbines
• Assault rifles
• Submachine guns and light machine guns

The United Nations defines light weapons as:
• Heavy machine guns
• Handheld under-barrel and mounted grenade launchers
• Portable antitank and antiaircraft guns
• Recoilless rifles
• Portable launchers of antitank and antiaircraft missile systems
• Mortars of less than 4.3 inches (100 mm) caliber

total number of firearms manufactured in the world. Approximately 30 percent of all arms are exported from the United States.

The spread of weapons has had many negative effects on certain areas of the world. Some areas that were already politically and economically unstable have become extremely dangerous because of it. The threat of danger even keeps away some necessary resources. Doctors, teachers, and resources such as food or medical supplies are desperately needed in many heavily armed areas. But it is often too dangerous to send the needed help. Or when help is sent, it is often commandeered by heavily armed gangs or insurgents. Without the basic needs of the people being met, the area can become stuck in violence and poverty with little hope for the future.

Another issue that contributes to this problem is the amount of money governments spend on weapons. Some governments spend more than 30 percent of their annual budget on arms. This leaves little money for development. Money that could be spent on education, poverty, hunger, and health care is spent on small arms instead.

A Somali man selling khat in Mogadishu

Mikhail Kalashnikov designed the AK-47 rifle.

FROM BOW AND ARROW
TO AK-47

*I*t is hard to imagine a time when there were no guns, bombs, missiles, or grenades. But it was not until the fifteenth century that firearms began to be used as the primary weapons of soldiers during warfare.

Though gunpowder was first discovered between 600 and 900 CE, no one determined how to control it for accuracy for hundreds of years. Fighting and hunting generally relied on human might and skill. Common weapons included spears, javelins, clubs, sharpened stones, and bows and arrows. With these types of weapons, fighters would thrust or hurl weapons at their targets. Technology in making weapons was based on creating tools that would be easier to move and control.

One precursor to firearms was the bow and arrow. It was the first weapon that allowed the user to shoot its target from a significant distance. Yet, even the bow and arrow required its shooter to possess a level of skill and strength. Eventually, people learned how to shoot lead balls at high speed, propelled by exploding gunpowder—and changed warfare forever.

Gunpowder

Gunpowder is a mixture of sulfur, potassium nitrate, arsenic disulphide, and honey. The combination of these four elements ignites when heated. At first, people did not know how to control the explosions that erupted when gunpowder was lit, so it was used only to create noise and drama at festivals and celebrations. European soldiers began to confine and direct it during the twelfth-century Crusades. Once they learned how to use it to propel a projectile toward a target, it became a weapon for killing enemies. Yet, warriors and soldiers still did not have total control over the explosion it created. It was often a danger to the shooter, especially since it was fired so close to the face.

The First Firearms

One of the first firearms invented was a long-barreled firearm called a harquebus that was developed in Europe. With this new technology, Italian soldiers were able to kill 6,000 Frenchmen in the battle of Pavia, Italy, in 1525. This upsurge in technology soon led to the Spanish-designed heavy musket. Yet, the musket had a disadvantage. It took time to reload the powder and ball after every shot. Then, in the nineteenth century, gunpowder was incorporated into the projectiles now called bullets. Guns could be reloaded quickly, and other advances increased the number of shots that could be fired before reloading. Modern-day rifles were quickly adapted to take advantage of this new technology, and the musket soon became obsolete.

Guns Change Warfare Forever

In the 1860s, the American Civil War was the first to take advantage of this new technology, and the effects were substantial. There was more death in a shorter period of time during this war than ever before. Approximately 175,000 Confederate soldiers died by gunshot between 1861 and 1863. It was during this period that machine guns were

*A four-year-old Palestinian boy displayed an AK-47 during
an anti-Israel and anti-United States rally organized
by the Palestinian Resistance in the southern Gaza Strip in 2002.*

developed, which could fire as many as 600 rounds per minute.

Yet the technological advances did not stop there. Between World War I and World War II, the United States developed a new generation of machine gun called the M1. The M1 was widely used by the US military and exported to European allies. However,

Mikhail Kalashnikov

Mikhail Kalashnikov was born in Siberia in 1919. As a soldier in the Soviet army, he spent many years perfecting the Kalashnikov rifle, the AK-47. Brilliantly designed, the Kalashnikov can be used in any weather or environment. It is inexpensive to make, fires rapidly, and is easy to maneuver and shoot. Despite its popularity, Kalashnikov never received any royalties for its sales, only Soviet honors.

He later said of the AK-47, "I'm proud of my invention but I'm sad that it is used by terrorists. I would prefer to have invented a machine that people could use and that would help farmers with their work—for example a lawnmower."[1]

it could not compete with the popularity of the AK-47, developed by Soviet soldier Mikhail Kalashnikov in 1944 during World War II. The AK-47, or "Kalashnikov," is still the most plentiful and widely used weapon in the world.

THE COLD WAR

The AK-47 experienced its rise in popularity during the Cold War and is now widely associated with the global arms trade. For nearly 50 years during the Cold War, from 1945 to 1991, the United States and the Soviet Union were enemies politically and economically. But this war was different. It was based on political maneuverings rather than outright warfare. Both the United States and the Soviet Union held secrets to the best leading weapons technology. They knew that their nuclear weaponry could destroy each other quickly, so they did not fight each other directly. Both feared a brutal bloodbath.

Yet both governments spent a great deal of money supporting the development of weapons technology. They wanted to maintain huge stockpiles of small and large arms for use by their own militaries and to trade with their allies in other countries. The United States would not fight the Soviets directly, but it would supply weapons to nations that did fight them or their allies.

US allies included Western European countries, such as the United Kingdom, France, and West Germany. Asian and Middle Eastern countries such as Israel, Japan, South Korea, Pakistan, India, and Saudi Arabia also became US

The AK-47

Currently, an estimated 70 to 100 million AK-47s exist worldwide. AK-47s or AK-derived assault rifles are listed in government arsenals in at least 82 countries. It is the most pervasive weapon of all time and has become a cultural icon. It is "the weapon that we think of when we think about internal conflicts or anti-colonialism. It's really become a part of the culture."[2] It has come to symbolize terrorism, insurgency, and criminal violence.

Three well-known terrorist groups use images of the AK-47 in their logos. In photos and video footage, Osama bin Laden and Saddam Hussein have often been shown with AK-47s. However, because of the weapon's overt link to terrorism, some governments seek to erase their country's connection to the AK-47. For example, the Mozambican parliament approved a law to remove the AK-47 from its flag and currency. "For many [Mozambicans] removing the gun from the flag is an important symbol of their country's commitment to peace," according to *The Arms Trade: A Beginner's Guide*.[3]

allies. Meanwhile, the Soviet Union counted East Germany, Poland, Hungary, North Korea, Yugoslavia, and several other countries in Eastern Europe and elsewhere as friends.

Arms trade among these countries was most often regulated by these alliances. A political and literal barrier known as the Iron Curtain separated the East and West and helped determine alliances. The partnerships developed during this Cold War period led to the development of many pathways that continue to mark the modern-day arms trade.

The Iron Curtain

The Iron Curtain figuratively describes the political barrier between the West and the East. A well-known symbol of this division was the Berlin Wall, a physical barrier that closed access from East Germany to West Berlin from 1961 to 1989. The Berlin Wall and other fortified and patrolled borders divided Western Europe from Eastern Europe. During the Cold War, there was almost no migration from the East to the West of the Iron Curtain. When the Berlin Wall finally fell in 1989, it symbolized unity between the East and the West and opened up new paths for commerce and trade, including weapons trade.

Post Cold War

The Soviet Union began to break up in the late 1980s, and the arms industry took a hit. Suddenly, the demand for military goods dropped considerably. Alliances lost much of their economic and political meaning. Former enemies were not as much of a threat. Between 1987 and 1997, arms production and expenditure fell approximately

The Berlin Wall, which acted as a border separating East and West Berlin, was officially opened on November 9, 1989.

30 percent. Production and spending did not pick up again until 2001 with the onset of wars in Afghanistan and, in 2003, Iraq.

By the time the Cold War ended completely in 1991, arms manufacturers were being forced to depart from the military strategies of their countries and move toward new business strategies. One new business strategy was called scenario setting.

With scenario setting, governments and arms manufacturers began considering new scenarios of conflict. What countries might need to arm themselves against others? Similarly, what countries would become new allies?

This approach to the arms industry also became tied to new markets in developing states in the Middle East, Africa, and Southeast Asia. These areas were also key locations where oil existed. Thus, the arms trade began intermingling with other industries—trading arms for drugs, diamonds, and other goods across the world.

These changes in the arms industry had several effects. Arms manufacturing companies began to acquire or merge with foreign companies. There were also new business opportunities for brokers who could negotiate arms sales between manufacturers and purchasers in different countries. In addition, the policies that the arms trade had formerly been based on had lost meaning, and few clear laws were available to replace the old policies. The process of spreading weapons rapidly throughout the world had begun. ⌐

US Marines confiscated many AK-47s in Baghdad, Iraq, in April 2003.

Mujahideen rebels ranged in the mountains of Afghanistan in 1980.

WEAPONS CHANGING
HANDS

uring its existence, a gun might travel from country to country, being used in one war after another. An AK-47 abandoned by the military in Afghanistan after the Cold War may have been used in the Bosnian War (1992–1995) and then in south-central Asia to arm Afghani terrorists by the early twenty-first century. Most firearms are almost indestructible and likely to outlive a soldier in battle. Even with use in multiple wars, the weapon rarely loses its power.

Weapons transfer from one region to another can occur by several different methods. A weapon could be transferred through trade between governments, trade through brokers, licensed production, black market trades, postwarfare abandonment, and pathways created during previous wars. Oftentimes, several different types of transactions take place before a weapon has completed the journey from manufacturer to end user. Legal and illegal processes are often used in combination.

TRAILS OF TRADE, TRAILS OF BLOOD

Weapons from previous conflicts can often lead to the spread of arms in certain regions. In the late 1970s and 1980s, the Soviet Union was at war with the mujahideen, the Islamic rebel fighters of Afghanistan. The Soviets were much better equipped than their opponents. Yet the guerilla warriors found ways to improve their position, including raiding Soviet supplies.

In 1989, arms dealers' shops in Pakistan sold many kinds of weapons.

The mujahideen's main source of weaponry eventually became the United States. The United States did not want to fight the Soviet Union directly. But it wanted to support Afghanistan in its stance against Communism. To that end, the United States supplied weapons to the guerilla warriors to indirectly fight the Soviets. This was the type of warfare common in the Cold War.

Yet in order to equip the Afghanis with weaponry, a path to the fighters needed to be forged. Afghanistan was landlocked; weapons needed to be transported through another nation to reach the mujahideen. So the bordering country of Pakistan became what is known as a transit state. A transit state is a channel through which weapons are moved in order to arrive at the recipient state. Pakistan supported the mujahideen's fight against Soviet Communism. It also has a coast on the Arabian Sea, so it was an ideal candidate for transiting weapons. The United States purchased weapons from countries such as China, Poland, Egypt, and Turkey. The weapons then entered and passed through Pakistan on their way to Afghanistan.

"Small arms almost always outlast the political relationships that existed between the original supplier and recipient, and one needs look no farther than the anti-US activities of Osama bin Laden and his network of the former Afghan freedom fighters to see how covert arms sales can come back to haunt the supplier nations."[1]
—*William Hartung of the World Policy Institute*

Millions of weapons entered Pakistan through this pipeline, and millions remained after the Cold War ended. These weapons have contributed to violence in the region since then.

These same weapons were used in warfare against American soldiers during the Afghanistan War following the September 11, 2001, attacks on the United States by al-Qaeda terrorists based in Afghanistan.

Though arms are traded between allied governments, political relationships often change over time. In the case of the United States arming Afghan rebels, weapons outlasted the once friendly relationship between them. This trail of trade between allies led to a trail of blood between them years later.

Controlling the Trade

Controlling the path weapons take from one user to another is difficult. Two attempts to control the spread of arms include government licenses and embargoes, or the forced stoppage of trade.

With licenses, governments can sell weapons to each other through an arrangement of licensed production. This means that a country purchases ready-to-assemble parts that can be put together in its own country. In other cases, a government might license the technology. The receiving government would acquire certain knowledge, or scientific expertise, to manufacture and assemble all the parts of the weapon.

Governments have also attempted to enforce embargoes to particular regions to control the spread of arms. For example, Afghanistan became riddled with terrorists and the abuse of arms during its civil war in the 1990s. Because the fighting and terror were out of control, the United Nations voted to impose an embargo on Afghanistan in 1996. The embargo has been revised since then, but it still stands.

CONTROLLING THE PEOPLE

Changes in government alliances is only one factor

Idi Amin, Killing, and Arms Trade

Ugandan dictator Idi Amin was legendary for his charismatic personality and his "blood lust." His loud, boisterous personality helped win the hearts of the Ugandan people. Yet, under his dictatorship from 1971 to 1979, a reign of death took hold. At least 200,000 Ugandans were killed.

Amin was said to have been afflicted by neurosyphilis, a disease that causes mental insanity. He became more violent and nightmarish in the later stages of his dictatorship. He is thought to have talked to the severed heads of victims. He stored the heads in freezers and fed their bodies to alligators in the Nile River. The story of Amin's horrifying regime was the basis of a novel and film entitled *The Last King of Scotland*.

Amin was also an active supporter of the Palestinian Liberation Organization (PLO), which he armed with SA-7 surface-to-air missiles. The Palestinian radical group had intended to take down an Israeli airliner, but the plan was discovered by Israeli intelligence. The perpetrators were arrested by Kenyan police near the airport.

The Nicaraguan Contra Embargo

Embargoes are well intentioned, yet they may do little more than set the stage for a new supplier to enter the market. This was the case when the United States cut off aid to the Nicaraguan contras fighting the Soviet-backed Sandinista government. The United States had secretly supported this large rebel group for years. At one point, the US government decided to cut off aid. Yet the contras still managed to obtain 10,000 Polish AK-47 rifles with $15 million from a separate source. These weapons were said to have traveled from the Bulgarian port of Burgas to an unknown country in Latin America before making their way to the contras.

contributing to the leaking of weapons onto the black market and illegal trading. When it comes to arms trade, controlling the actions and motives of individual participants is extremely difficult. Corruption is a major problem. Weapons may be sold directly by soldiers. Military officers in Israel were found to have knowingly sold weapons to Palestinian fighters even though those same weapons would be used against them in battle. Further, corrupt government officials may arm or trade with unsavory partners, such as terrorists, in order to promote their own regimes. In the 1970s and 1980s, Libyan dictator Mu'ammar al-Gadhafi and Ugandan dictator Idi Amin armed Palestinian terrorists with missiles meant to take down Israeli airliners. These regimes strongly opposed Israel's policies toward Palestinians yet were reluctant to engage the Israeli military directly.

Contra soldiers marched the streets of Nicaragua in 1989.

So they turned to other military agents to keep the
pressure on Israel. By openly supporting the popular
Palestinian cause, they sought to divert attention
from economic hardships in their own countries.

Controlling arms trade and controlling the
actions of individuals involved is difficult. Weapons

might enter a country through legal channels such as imports and licensed production. Yet there is no guarantee that they will not make their way to the black market later. This problem is not limited to warring or poor, developing countries. In the United States, 500,000 weapons—mainly handguns—are burglarized from homes and resold on the black market every year. In South Africa, an average of 43 guns were stolen every day, totaling 15,497, between 2004 and 2005.

Clearly, arms travel across legal and illegal lines fairly easily—and rich and poor lines too. So what is the role of the law in preventing proliferation of arms and black market sales?

Former Ugandan dictator Idi Amin armed Palestinian terrorists in order to weaken the Israeli regime.

Arms dealer Viktor Bout was held in Bangkok, Thailand, before being extradited to the United States in 2010.

The Role of the Law

hotos of AK-47 rifles strapped to the bodies of terrorists in underdeveloped countries abound. But where did these weapons come from? Are they obtained through legal or illegal channels? And how do countries that are extremely poor in sustainable resources become rich in arms? The reality is that many weapons in the hands of the most dangerous terrorists, insurgents, and political dictators are exported from the leading—and some of the richest—countries including the United States. At least 550 million known firearms exist around the world today. Many of these weapons were acquired through legal channels. The arms trade industry includes approximately $5 billion per year in transactions. Most of the transactions—approximately $4 billion—are legal.

The legal aspect of the arms trade is best understood when divided into three main categories: legal trade, illicit trade, and the gray market. Legal trade follows UN arms embargoes policies. This type of trade might involve a country sending arms to troops in a foreign country

Where Arms Begin and End

As of 2010, more than 600 companies in 95 countries manufacture weapons legally. The United States has been the leader in manufacturing and sales for the past several decades, followed by Russia and China. Leading arms manufacturers include Lockheed Martin, Boeing, and Euro-American conglomerate BAE Systems. In 2007, Lockheed Martin's total sales reached $38.5 billion.

The top importers of firearms are China, India, the Middle East, South Korea, and Greece. Between 2004 and 2008, 37 percent of all US weapons exports went to the Middle East. This included 5,000 guided bombs and 207 combat aircrafts.

under the approval and in full compliance with
UN regulations. Usually the UN implements arms
embargoes on countries that are known to violate
human rights or those with undemocratic regimes.

Illicit trade clearly violates national or
international laws. A firearm that has been stolen
and resold or a bomb that has been illegally
manufactured and sold are examples of illicit or
black market trade. The demand for arms obtained
through the black market has increased as the United
Nations has implemented an increasing number of
embargoes in unstable areas.

Gray market trade is the most common form
of trade that results in insurgents or terrorists
becoming end users of weapons. In the gray market,
dealers or governments can work around policies
and exploit certain loopholes. For example, a
government may endorse the trade of weapons
that violates international law but does not violate
national laws of exporting or importing countries.
Experts believe the gray market produces a higher
volume and dollar value of sales than the black
market.

Loopholes in the Law

The story of arms dealer Leonid Minin shows how the gray market can facilitate trade that does not comply with international policies yet avoid prosecution. In 2000, Minin was arrested in a raid at the Europa Hotel in Italy where 1,500 falsified documents were confiscated. It turned out that Minin had sold more than 200 tons (181 tonnes) of small arms, light weapons, and ammunition to Charles Taylor, the dictator of Liberia, while the African country was under a UN arms embargo. Further, Minin had brokered weapons trade to the Revolutionary United Front in Sierra Leone while that West African country was under a UN embargo. Despite Minin's obvious involvement in these sales, he was released in 2002 due to lax Italian laws. Because he had not brought the weapons into Italy at any point during the trades,

Gun Violence in Mexico with US Weapons

Weapons manufactured in the United States have been used in a significant number of criminal incidents in Mexico. The cardinal of Guadalajara, Juan Jesus Posadas Ocampo, was assassinated in 1993 with a gun manufactured in the United States. Presidential candidate Luis Donaldo Colosio was killed in 1994 in Tijuana with a Taurus pistol that had been smuggled into Mexico from the United States.

he technically had not broken Italian law and would not be held accountable.

GOVERNMENT USE OF BROKERS
AND THE GRAY MARKET

The gray market is exploited not only by individuals and corrupt governments. Many stable governments use brokers to engage in gray market trades to help keep certain sales secret. In some cases, the government sells arms to a broker, and the broker supplies the arms to a guerilla organization to fight on behalf of the government's military. Brokers can help governments trade arms and other goods quickly because they are familiar with the trading terrain and have established trading partners.

In some cases, brokers make themselves so valuable to governments that they become protected from imprisonment for illegal activity. Perhaps the most famous broker was Viktor Bout. Despite the fact that Bout's involvement in illegal trade was well established, his ties to various governments allowed him to live freely for many years. He is said to have profited at least $50 million from sales to the Taliban in Afghanistan during the 1990s. The

United States and Britain used his companies to transport cargo in Iraq.

Operating in the Gray Zone

Brokers rely on the loopholes of national versus international laws to remain within the gray zone. They frequently move operations from one country to another in order to stay ahead of the law or escape it and work with a number of other key players, including pilots, financiers, freight forwarders, and corrupt government officials. The

Viktor Bout

Known as the "Merchant of Death," Viktor Bout is the world's most famous arms dealer. Born in Tajikistan in 1967 and raised in New York City, Bout speaks six languages. He has become famous for his ability to manipulate the gray market to trade arms. The 2005 film *Lord of War* depicts Bout's career of dealing arms to all sides of civil conflicts in the warring countries of Sudan, Sierra Leone, Rwanda, Liberia, and Libya. Despite being accused by the United Nations of violating arms embargoes in several conflict regions, Bout managed to live freely in Moscow, Russia, for many years.

Bout operated several air charter companies, including Air Cess. His aircraft business allowed him to do legal business with many companies while transporting arms. He made millions of dollars from contracts with US companies such as FedEx and Kellogg Brown and Root. He operated his air charters out of the United Arab Emirates but regularly changed registration of his 50 aircraft in order to conduct business.

Bout was arrested in a sting operation between Thailand and the United States in 2008 when he attempted to sell weapons to the Revolutionary Armed Forces of Colombia (FARC) rebels. Bout was imprisoned in Bangkok for more than two years. In 2010, he was extradited to the United States to stand trial on weapons trafficking and terrorism charges.

A gun and knife show in White Plains, New York, June 2010

brokers obtain fake documents, including passports
and end-user certificates. In one case, fake Nigerian
end-user certificates allowed 200 tons (181 tonnes) of

guns and ammo to be transported from Monrovia, Liberia, to Belgrade, Serbia, between May and August of 2002. Similarly, in 1997 in Africa, weapons disguised as humanitarian aid were easily transported from Zaire to Burundi.

Corrupt and negligent governments often turn a blind eye and fail to check documents properly. This allows traders to fairly easily pass through territories with arms that will soon enter the black market. Some officials might even provide export licenses in exchange for bribes.

Gray market transactions occur frequently because it is often difficult to distinguish a legal trade from an illegal one. Governments use the same trade routes—many of which were established during the Cold War—that are used by brokers and illegal traders.

US Law Strict on Exports, Easy in Homeland

National laws vary widely from country to country. The United States has strict regulations on arms exports. These regulations require licenses for exports and oversight of state transfers and disposal of weapons. Brokering laws also apply regardless of where a broker conducts business.

Yet, despite strong national regulations on export and brokering in the United States, it is relatively easy for private US citizens to purchase firearms. Some of those firearms find their way to Mexico and Canada, countries that hold stricter regulations on firearm purchases. Critics of US law around firearm ownership point out that 80 percent of recovered criminal arms in Mexico were manufactured in the United States. Similarly, approximately 50 percent of criminal arms recovered in Canada originated in the United States.

The National Rifle Association (NRA), an organization established in 1871, has been a strong advocate for the right of US citizens to keep and bear arms. Since the 1970s, the NRA has dedicated much of its effort to safeguarding the rights of American gun owners. However, the ease of purchasing guns in the United States has also inadvertently helped arm terrorists. Several members of the terrorist organization al-Qaeda lived in the United States in order to acquire guns. Gun kits that can be ordered through the mail and gun shows that provide opportunities to network with dealers are just two ways that terrorists have gained access to the American firearms market.

In 2000, Ali Boumelhem was convicted for conspiring to sell weapons to the terrorist group Hezbollah. Boumelhem was a convicted felon, yet he was able to purchase the weapons at Michigan gun shows. The law did not require sellers at Michigan gun shows to conduct background checks.

THE CHALLENGE OF INTERNATIONAL LAW

Clearly, the reliance on national law and lack of enforceable international law contribute to gray market arms trade and the illegal spread of weapons. However, it has been difficult for diplomats to draft a meaningful international treaty that leading exporters will support. Leadings exporters include Russia, Germany, France, and the United States.

International laws are often at odds with the objectives of individual

Arms Linked to Crime

The presence of military weapons in unstable regions has a direct impact on the types of crimes committed and the death rate. In Nicaragua, 44 percent of crimes committed involved military weapons in 2000. The percentage of murders by firearms increased from 55 percent in the years 1990 to 1995 to 75 percent in 1999 due to the influx of small arms. In Honduras, firearms were involved in 82 percent of the deaths of young people in 2001, and 36 percent involved AK-47 rifles. By comparison, only 25 percent of 582 murders in Canada in 2002 involved firearms.

governments. The United States, for example, has become more resistant to the international community imposing on its foreign policy since the September 11, 2001, attacks. Such resistance and the intermixing of other industries with the arms trade have made it difficult for the global community to come to an agreement on international arms trade law. ⌐

Visitors crowded the aisles at the Great Western Gun Show
in Pomona, California, in 1999.

Former Liberian president Charles Taylor provided guerilla groups with weapons.

GUNS AND DIAMONDS

An attraction to guns—and the power they offer—has been around for centuries. But the glitter and gleam of jewels has been around even longer. Illicit gun trade is often tied to other illicit trade, including diamonds, oil, and drugs. And the amount some will pay for these items is high.

In the 1990s, the Revolutionary United Front (RUF), a guerilla organization in Sierra Leone, used the diamond industry to fund its war against the central government. Through illegal diamond sales and support from Charles Taylor's regime in Liberia, the RUF purchased weapons that were used in a reign of terror against the people of Sierra Leone.

After the Cold War, the National Union for the Total Independence of Angola (UNITA) rebel forces raised funds through illicit arms trade with the diamond industry. On the other side of the fighting, the Angolan government used profits from offshore oil deposits in order to keep its weapons arsenals stocked in defense against UNITA. UNITA earned an estimated $3.7 billion in diamond sales between 1992 and 1997. Similarly, in Colombia, corrupt government officials and guerillas have profited illegally from the cocaine trade since the 1970s. This lucrative business has fueled the arms trade throughout the country.

The lines between legal and illicit trade continue to blur as high-profit industries mingle together.

The situation is further complicated by trade routes.
Legal industries and humanitarian organizations
often use the same trade routes as the illegal arms, diamond, and drug trade. It can be easy to smuggle illicit trade in the same cargo as legal trade.

Charles Taylor and the Sierra Leone Diamond Trade

Liberian dictator Charles Taylor is considered by many to be responsible for many of the horrors endured in West Africa from 1991 to his indictment in 2003. Approximately 250,000 people died in the war between the Liberian government and Taylor's insurgency.

Taylor began supporting the Revolutionary United Front guerilla group in Sierra Leone in 1991, six years before he became president. He provided the rebels with weapons in exchange for diamonds. In order to mine the diamonds for the exchange, the rebels kidnapped thousands of civilians and forced them into slavery as diamond miners. Many were brutally abused and killed.

Taylor also ran a timber industry that operated as a front for the trade of arms and diamonds. Brokers in China sent arms through the Liberian ports, which were controlled by the Oriental Timber Company and Maryland Wood Processing and backed by the military.

Taylor was indicted in 2003 on 17 counts of war crimes, human rights crimes, unlawful killing, sexual violence, forced conscription of child soldiers, forced labor, and attacks on UN peacekeepers. He fled but was eventually caught and convicted in 2006 of 11 of the charges.

His reign has been described as "a relentless campaign of sadistic, wanton violence unimaginable to those unfamiliar with . . . [Taylor's] capacity to visit the abyss."[1]

BUDGETS AND PRICES

Arms trade has been a high-dollar business for many years. In 2006, the United States spent $11.8 billion on weaponry research and development. In the United Kingdom, an annual budget of $17.5 million allows politicians to visit arms trading partners to promote sales of weapons from the United Kingdom.

When Saddam Hussein's regime was overthrown in 2003, unguarded weapons flooded the streets of Iraq. On average, prices of firearms dropped by 50 percent or more because they were so plentiful and easy to obtain. Suddenly, an AK-47 could be purchased for $200 instead of $600.

The Impact of Global Trade

Arms can be traded for a number of goods, making their impact on the global economy significant. For example, arms trade has a direct effect on jobs. Trading weapons for commodities might help major exporters such as the United States establish relationships with foreign countries. It may even help bring jobs to those countries. However, as much as $2.3 billion or as many as 4,200 American jobs within a five-year period are lost in such arrangements.

Many people believe that slowing the arms industry would result in lost jobs. However, one study showed that the number of jobs available to civilians would increase by 27 percent should arms exporting be reduced by half.

Exporting Country	Total Value of Exported Arms	Countries Exported To
United States	$31.8 billion	Japan Colombia Netherlands Bahrain Egypt
United Kingdom	$8.7 billion	Afghanistan Turkey Saudi Arabia Brazil Pakistan
Bulgaria	$5.3 billion	Iraq
Germany	$5 billion	Saudi Arabia United States Latvia Switzerland Malaysia
Italy	$4.6 billion	Switzerland Mexico United States

The top five exporting countries' global transfers of small arms in 2006

ARMS EXHIBITIONS

Some of the most dramatic examples of how the arms trade functions as a global economic force occur at arms exhibitions. Filled with the newest technology in weaponry, these exhibitions are attended by arms manufacturers, operators, dealers, private owners, and military defense experts and personnel. Exporters and importers from warring countries frequently interact and negotiate deals at arms exhibitions, using brokers to conceal their transactions. Like the weapons they deal in, brokers generally operate without political alliances. Rather, they serve the needs of those who will pay the most, whether respected governments, dictatorships, or terrorists.

Arms manufacturing declined between the end of the Cold War and 2000. However, arms exhibitions regained momentum with the onset of the Afghanistan and Iraq wars in the early years of the twenty-first century due to higher demand among the United States and its allies.

The Arms Trade Effect on Jobs

Some argue the current level of arms manufacturing should be maintained. Proponents state that it contributes to the number of domestic jobs. They also argue that arms producers are skilled in a specific craft and could not be easily retrained to produce another type of product.

Critics of this argument note that arms manufacturing jobs are actually relatively few in number and have decreased steadily over the past few decades. Critics also argue that many arms manufacturers have a wide variety of engineering skills that could be applied to many different industries if not devoted to the production of arms. In addition, they have questioned why the government should protect jobs in this particular sector but not in other industries.

Thirty major arms fairs are held every year. Britain's largest arms exhibition, the DSEi, or Defence and Security Equipment International, has drawn the attention of many campaigners who are interested in changing the nature of the arms industry. Just five days after the September 11, 2001, terrorist attacks on the United States, the DSEi held the largest British arms exhibition ever. The success of the weapons show provided evidence to some critics that "[s]ince 9/11, the War on Terror has been very good for business."[2] Representatives from the United States, Israel, and 14 Arab nations were in attendance. Author Gideon Burrows described it this way: "Sworn enemies shopped side by side for weapons to use against one another."[3] Meanwhile, hundreds of protestors rallied in opposition to the exhibition.

TRADE AND LOCAL ECONOMIES

Many experts argue that government spending on arms has indirectly stunted development in various regions around the world. Large percentages of government budgets have been spent on arms. For example, in 1985, before the Cold War ended, Mozambique spent 38 percent of its total budget on weaponry. Iran spent 34 percent. El Salvador, Ethiopia, and Nicaragua hovered around 30 percent. In many of these countries, very little money was left to help alleviate pressing socioeconomic issues such as poverty, hunger, education, child death rates, the environment, and health care. Many of these countries still have massive, growing debt because of overspending on arms.

A GROWING ISSUE

The impact of arms trade on the global economy can also be measured

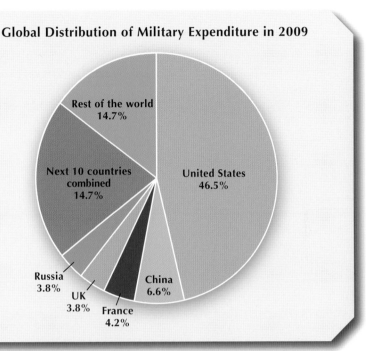

Global Distribution of Military Expenditure in 2009

Rest of the world
14.7%

Next 10 countries
combined
14.7%

United States
46.5%

Russia
3.8%

UK
3.8%

France
4.2%

China
6.6%

*The United States had the greatest percentage
of military expenditure in 2009.*

in social terms. In certain circumstances, some people and governments value their weapons more than anything else, including food, supplies, or cash. Weapons control under these circumstances can be very difficult.

Weapons control is further complicated because parts of weapons are now manufactured in multiple places. At one time, weapons were commonly built from start to finish in the same factory. Now, pieces come from many different industrial plants, from multiple countries, to finally be assembled in one place. This has led many experts on the arms trade to include many different types of tools under the umbrella of arms. This could include everything from ammunition to nonexplosive torture devices. Some even count people as part of the arms trade. For example, mercenaries or private armies are paid to battle. Thus, their human bodies are literally purchased as weapons.

Clearly, the arms trade is vast and underregulated. Governments have not been quick to enforce control on small arms. More than 200 governments, hundreds of insurgents, thousands of organized criminal groups, and hundreds of millions of individuals possess small arms and light weapons. What could seem like a small issue has loomed larger and larger for the last 30 years. ⌐

*A selection of ammunition on display at the Defence and Security
Equipment International in London in 2005*

Members of the Hezbollah guerrilla group in Lebanon hold a large model of a Kalashnikov assault rifle alongside a young boy carrying a toy gun.

SMALL ARMS, BIG PROBLEMS

W eapons come in all shapes and sizes. They can range from knives to machetes to torture equipment to land mines to bombs. News coverage of arms trade often focuses on the larger, more obvious weapons, such as weapons of mass destruction. Yet the issues of small arms can create more extensive and far-reaching problems than the threat of mass destruction. In this case, a small package can create big problems.

One problem leading to the issue of small arms is that small arms and light weapons are difficult to track. Years of poor management of weapons arsenals have put weapons in the hands of people all over the world. There are more than 230 million firearms in the United States. That equals 84 guns for every 100 people. Civilians own a much higher percentage of firearms than police or military. The whereabouts of these weapons are even less known. In the United States, civilians own 98 percent of all firearms, compared to 2 percent military ownership and 0.3 percent police ownership. Similar percentage breakdowns exist in poor countries and wealthy countries.

"Small arms may be the most commonly used and the most deadly of all armaments, but they have never received the degree of attention lavished upon major conventional weapons, much less weapons of mass destruction."[1]
—*Small Arms Survey*

Weapons of Mass Destruction

Weapons of mass destruction (WMD) has been identified as an over-used and somewhat inaccurate term. Fear of WMD became especially strong after the September 11, 2001, attacks, when Iraq was believed to hold such weapons. Though the United States and the United Kingdom invaded Iraq in 2003 in search of WMD, none were ever found.

Weapons of mass destruction are nuclear weapons. In two cases, nuclear weapons have been used. Both were American weapons the US military dropped on Japan during World War II to devastating effect. Countries known to possess nuclear weapons are the United States, Russia, the United Kingdom, France, China, India, Pakistan, and North Korea.

The issues surrounding the proliferation of small arms are worsened by some governments. Until the turn of the twenty-first century, the problem of uncontrolled small arms trade was unclear to many nations. Even with that knowledge now available, some countries remain unwilling to create and enforce stricter small arms controls.

Some countries are not equipped to properly manage the spread of firearms. Some nations have no money or military to guard their arsenals. Others may not take action because lost and stolen small arms are inexpensive to replace. Small arms are also perceived to pose a smaller threat because they are unlikely to cause significant damage to major infrastructures. Additionally, many governments have kept poor records of their arms inventories.

SECRETS AND ARMS

Governments refusing to reveal information about their arsenals of small arms also contribute to the spread of weapons. They argue that keeping this information private enhances security. Some leaders feel that opening up information about stockpiles could lead to unwanted scrutiny if their country is deemed to have too many. On the other hand, a country that has less could be seen as weak and easy to attack.

The illicit trade of torture equipment is one sector of small arms some governments want to keep secret. Some governments are suspected of not only underreporting the weapons they import or hold but of secretly producing weapons. Much media attention has been paid to the nuclear program in Iran throughout the first decade of the twenty-first century. While the Iranian government claims

Police Gun Ownership in the United States

Not only are US police officers armed at a far lower percentage than civilians, their weapons are not as advanced. Instead of automatic rifles and shotguns used by civilians, police use pistols. They must follow protocols and regulations, relying largely on nonlethal weapons such as stun devices, batons, and pepper spray. Thus, many police are unofficially encouraged to carry backup personal weapons, such as handguns, in order to protect themselves.

that research and development has been aimed at supporting a civilian energy program, skeptics note that the same technology could be used to develop nuclear weapons. Nuclear weapons development in Iran could upset global security if other countries nearby, such as Saudi Arabia, Egypt, and Syria, felt pressured to develop similar technology. The already conflict-ridden region could rapidly become even more violent.

The International Atomic Energy Agency (IAEA) of the UN has investigated Iran's nuclear program. Though no concrete evidence has resulted from the IAEA's investigations, intelligence experts still suspect Iran of nuclear weapons development. Iran's tendency to be secretive and conceal information has only led to more suspicion, media attention, and fear.

Despite the reluctance of governments to share information about their own arms, the fear of weapons of mass destruction has led to more openness and disclosure. Many legislators hope that new attention to the issue will lead to policies that not only help control nuclear weapons and weapons of mass destruction but also do a better job of curbing the spread of small arms and light weapons.

An Afghan victim of a land mine walked with his new artificial leg at the International Committee of the Red Cross (ICRC) Orthopaedic Center in Kabul, Afghanistan, in March 2010.

LAND MINES

Since the mid-1990s, land mines have received media and legislative attention. A land mine is implanted in the ground and explodes when the weight of a vehicle or troop passes over it. Land mines have been identified by many campaigners as a violation of human rights. Fortunately, an important treaty was negotiated that has helped control land mine usage quite a bit. In December 1997, the Mine

Ban Treaty was signed by 122 governments. This has helped reduce land mine stockpiles from 260 million in the mid-1990s to 176 million in 2008.

Unfortunately, the treaty does not have the support of the United States, China, Russia, Egypt, Finland, India, Israel, Pakistan, and 29 other countries. Burma, Russia, and several non-state groups in the Middle East and South America continue to use land mines. Furthermore, certain weapons, such as cluster bombs that are

Torture Equipment

Torture equipment and training in torture techniques is part of the arms trade. Part of the reason this trade is difficult to regulate is that some equipment such as batons, handcuffs, and leg shackles are widely used in law enforcement and are considered legitimate. However, other devices, such as restraint chairs, have almost no purpose other than for torture. At least a few individual cases have drawn more attention to the spread of these weapons.

Sandy Mitchell, a British anesthetic technician, worked at the Saudi Security Forces Hospital in Riyadh, Saudi Arabia. In December 2000, he was arrested and accused of a terrorist bombing. He was held in the "Confession Factory," where he was severely tortured and restrained by shackles for three years. After he was released, Mitchell was diagnosed with post-traumatic stress disorder. The equipment used to torture Mitchell was manufactured in Britain and led to a ban on the export of torture devices.

At the 2007 International Fire and Security Exhibition and Conference (IFSEC) in Birmingham, United Kingdom, a salesman openly marketed an electroshock weapon designed to deliver painful volts of electricity to a victim's sensitive body parts. The loud machine and the flash of light it gave off made it obvious to anyone walking by the exhibit. The salesman was arrested and deported.

dropped from aircraft, are not included in the treaty. Many cluster bombs do not explode on impact and remain implanted in the ground until they are disturbed. These have caused an enormous amount of damage since they were first introduced in World War II. As many as 50 million cluster bombs were dropped during the Gulf War in the early 1990s, which resulted in 1,600 deaths and 2,500 injuries over the next several years.

ATTITUDE

Attitude toward the arms trade is one barrier to stopping the spread of small arms. Some feel the problem has gotten so big that any effort to try to stop it would be useless. Critics of the global arms trade argue that wealthy countries do not care about the spread of arms to poor and troubled regions where the local people will use them on each other.

"Landmines are indiscriminate because a landmine is triggered by its victim, whether military or civilian. Landmines are inhumane because they inflict brutal injuries and have disastrous long-term consequences."[2]
—*International Campaign to Ban Landmines*

Instead, they argue, governments only worry about weapons that might take down commercial airlines filled with people from wealthy Western countries. If such critics are indeed correct, then governments are playing a dangerous game. The presence of small firearms has a much greater impact than death and destruction in countries overrun by them. It affects industries and foreign relations on a global scale.

A 2008 protest in Turkey raises issues related to the arms trade,
such as torture and corruption.

A Stinger missile trainer helps fighters locate targets and launch missiles.

Man–Portable Missiles

*D*uring the mid–1980s, the Soviet Union was at war against Afghanistan. The Afghan rebels, the mujahideen, were a tough group, even nightmarish in their brutality. One dead Soviet soldier was found wrapped inside out in his own skin. Some mujahideen were known to cover themselves in gasoline and hurl their burning bodies against Soviet trucks. Still, they had old weapons that were no match for their Soviet opponents. The Soviets had Mi-24 Hind helicopters. These were 55.8 feet (17 m) in length and 13 feet (4 m) in height. Their guns could shoot hundreds of bullets per minute. Some Afghanis described these aircraft as monsters, killing in droves. So many Afghanis were dead and dying that even the hospitals in neighboring Pakistan were overrun with injured Afghanis. If the Afghanis were going to have a chance in this war, they needed something powerful enough to shoot the Hind helicopters out of the sky.

THE STINGER MISSILE

Enter the Stinger missile, or man-portable air-defense system (MANPADS), at only 6.6 feet (2 m) long and weighing just 44 pounds (20 kilograms). The missile was capable of traveling 1,500 miles per hour (2,414 km/h). It could follow the path of its target midflight until it made contact and exploded. The Stinger was so powerful it could take down a $200 million aircraft.

The United States began supplying the mujahideen with these power-loaded missiles. With shipments coordinated by the Central Intelligence Agency (CIA), the mujahideen started receiving the missiles by the truckloads. Weapons were also imported from other countries that feared the spread of Soviet Communism too. In 1987, Saudi Arabia matched the United States' contribution for a total of $630 million worth of arms. Japanese pickup trucks and Turkish small arms and ammo flooded the area. Mine-clearing equipment and other light weapons came from China. Armed with these new weapons, the mujahideen quickly regained their morale and began to combat the Soviets. The Soviets withdrew from the territory in 1989. By that time, the rebels had shot down 269 of their aircraft.

A Terrorist's Delight

MANPADS have become so iconic among insurgents that they have been referred to as a "terrorist's delight." The MANPADS were so desirable that Colombian guerillas were willing to pay $1 million for a system. This is equivalent to the salaries of 1,300 of their members. The missiles are small, which makes them easy to use and to smuggle. They cost a mere $2,000 on the black market.

ONE WAR LEADS TO ANOTHER

But war was not over for the mujahideen, who quickly began using the foreign-supplied weapons against their own people. Much to the chagrin of the US government, the mujahideen demonstrated their support for Iraqi dictator Saddam Hussein, a known enemy of the United States. Celebration over the Afghani victory was replaced by widespread fear over the missiles that now occupied the region.

The mujahideen quickly dismissed the US request that the missiles not be dispersed. One Afghani commander said simply, "We do sell some of your weapons. We are doing it for the day when your country decides to abandon us, just as you abandoned Vietnam and everyone else you deal with."[1]

Missiles Around the World

Just as many opponents of the missile exports to Afghanistan had feared, the weapons quickly spread into anti-American hands during and after Soviet occupation. Hundreds of weapons disappeared and were sold. As Arizonan Senator Dennis DeConcini said, "Now our worst enemies may have one of our best weapons in one of the most volatile regions of the world."[2] The missiles were seized by both

Psychological Impact of Stinger Missiles

In the Californian warehouse where the FIM-92 Stinger missiles were built, a large motto was displayed across the wall that read, "If it flies, it dies."[3] Stingers had such a profound psychological effect on the mujahideen that the term "Stinger Effect" was dubbed. Each Hind helicopter that fell boosted the mujahideen morale and weakened the Soviets.

Many Afghan guerrillas obtained US-made Stinger antiaircraft missiles.

Soviets and Iranians, with the promise from the
Iranian ambassador to "use all the means we have
to defend" ourselves against the US military.[4] The
weapons also spread to other insurgents and rebel
groups. These included the Chechen separatists,
Algerian fundamentalists, Kurdish rebels in
Turkey, Liberation Tigers of the brutal Sri Lankan
insurgency group Tamil Eelam, and the Taliban of
Afghanistan, who obtained hundreds of Stingers.

Yet Soviet-made MANPADS spread even more
rapidly around the globe. The Irish Republican
Army (IRA) received multiple Soviet SA-7s in

addition to 120 tons (109 tonnes) of weaponry from Libya. In 1987, the French seized 150 tons (136 tonnes) of weaponry on its way from Libya to the IRA. Soviet soldiers also stole many from their own arsenals to sell for a profit. The Soviet SA-7 missiles migrated to the arsenals of 11 of the 14 non-state groups known to also possess MANPADS.

THE US GOVERNMENT'S INVOLVEMENT IN MISSILE TRADE

The number of missiles in the hands of enemies of the United States grew rapidly. Some questioned why the United States had sent them so freely to Afghanistan. In previous years, the US government had shown more caution when President Ronald Reagan proposed sending missiles to Saudi Arabia.

Reagan had proposed this weapon transfer for a number of reasons. He viewed Saudi Arabia as "the keystone of our strategic interests in the Gulf."[5] He wanted to build a long-term relationship with the Saudis.

Failures in Missile Technology Development

Although MANPADS are often considered to be some of the most technologically impressive weapons, a considerable amount of money has gone into developing failed missile technology. The United States spent $44 million on British Blowpipes in 1992, which was a disaster according to Mohammad Yousaf, an Afghanistan expert in the Pakistani intelligence service. Thirteen of these missiles were fired at Soviet aircrafts and missed their targets. The Soviet Strela missiles were similarly weak. Only 3 percent hit their targets.

Why Sell Weapons to the Saudis?

Those in favor of selling weapons to Saudi Arabia argued that if the United States did not sell to the Saudis, someone else would. US Representative Mel Levine critiqued this argument:

"For nearly two decades, the United States has been almost reflexively granting Saudi arms requests, but our policy has neither yielded Saudi support for key United States initiatives, nor resulted in Saudi cooperation in advancing United States security interests in the Middle East."[6]

It was assumed that the best way to do that would be to export missiles because the Saudis would need to continue importing parts, weapons upgrades, and even training from the United States. With this exchange of weapons, the United States would have a greater influence over Saudi decisions about defense and foreign policies. Reagan thought the missiles would help decrease Iran's threat to Saudi Arabia and Persian Gulf oil tankers. Finally, he did not want to sever ties with Saudi leaders by refusing to sell missiles. To the Saudis, that would have been seen as an insult.

Reagan's initial request to sell missiles to Saudi Arabia was rejected outright by Congress in 1984. He responded by leasing a handful of missiles to the Saudi royal family for an exhibition. Congress readily agreed to this. Yet when Reagan proposed to sell 1,200 missiles to the Saudis, his request was again rejected. The battle between Congress and the president culminated when Reagan exercised his right to waive Congressional notification

requirements. He did not have to get approval
from Congress if the situation was an emergency.
So Reagan sent an emergency shipment of 200
launchers and 400 missiles to the Saudis—a move
that was widely
criticized by
legislators. After
Reagan sent
the emergency
shipment to Saudi
Arabia, he made a
few more attempts
to send more
missiles. But he
finally gave up his
fight.

Congress
approached missile
distribution to
Saudi Arabia with
much more caution
than to Afghanistan
a few years later.
The US legislative
process does help

MANPADS Threats Spur Legislation

Missiles have had a unique ability to cause panic and even chaos in multiple examples around the world. A fear of missiles possessed by the Sudanese government prevented agencies from delivering relief to millions of Sudanese refugees in 1990. Experts believe that the missile attack that killed Rwandan President Juvenal Habyarimana spurred the horrific Rwandan genocide of 1994, during which 800,000 were killed in months.

The US Congress began to acknowledge the need to take legislative action on the arms trade along with the threat of terrorist missile attacks in the early twenty-first century. Congressman John Mica, chairman of the House Aviation Subcommittee, explained the seriousness of the situation:

I went into the meeting somewhat skeptical of, one, the threat; and two, whether we had the ability to deal in a technological fashion with the threat. . . . I came out convinced that this is probably one of the most serious challenges that we face. . . . I don't lose sleep over many things that I deal with and I've dealt with a lot since September 11, but I can tell you since that hearing I have lost some sleep.[7]

control the spread of arms. Yet weapons spread easily, and exporters have very limited control of arms once the weapons have left their home base.

Control through Legislation

In some ways, the threat of MANPADS has been the most significant driving force behind many of the current initiatives to change the scope of the global arms trade. One of the most meaningful pieces of US legislation regarding MANPADS was developed during the Clinton administration. The legislation was called Elements for Export Controls of Man-Portable Air Defense Systems. This became the first international agreement to help develop more control in the exports of MANPADS.

As missiles have increasingly fallen into the hands of terrorists, governments have become more willing to work together on international agreements to crack down on unlawful trading of missiles. As more lives have been lost, governments have resorted to other methods to help buy back some control. ‿

A Liberian United for Reconciliation and Democracy (LURD) rebel fighter
opening the ammunition case of a mortar, a type of firearm

*The Afghan government surrendered Soviet missiles
to the United Nations in 2004.*

BUYING BACK CONTROL

ifty-two passengers boarded Air Rhodesia
flight number 825 on September 3, 1978.
The passengers had no idea they would soon become
victims of a brutal attack that would change the way
the world viewed missiles. They were headed from

Kariba to Salisbury—a city now called Harare—in former Rhodesia, which has since become Zimbabwe. Out of nowhere, one side of the airplane burst into flames. Not knowing what had hit the plane, pilot John Hood pulled an emergency landing. The plane crashed to the ground, hitting a ditch, rolling, and breaking into several pieces. Only 18 passengers emerged alive.

While five passengers searched for help, 13 others waited at the site of the crash. They huddled together, shocked but relieved they had survived. Their relief, however, would be short-lived. They were surrounded by members of the Rhodesian Patriotic Front, a Black Nationalist movement that was supported by the Soviets in their mission to overthrow Rhodesia's white-dominated government. The rebels opened fire on the 13 passengers, killing all but three who escaped. Word quickly traveled that the passengers of flight 825 had been the victims of the first surface-to-air missile attack on civilians traveling by commercial airline.

Flight to Paris

In 1996, a plane on a flight bound for Paris exploded off the coast of Long Island, New York, killing 230 people. The media was filled with speculation that the crash could have been caused by a missile attack. Though no evidence of an attack was ever uncovered, the growing threat that missiles were at large and could be used against Americans was partially responsible for the development of legislation such as Elements for Export Controls of Man-Portable Air Defense Systems.

MISSILE PANIC

Flight 825 was a frightening wake-up call to the world. People soon realized that missiles would not just be used in areas of conflict. They could easily target civilians and commercial aircraft all around the world. The panic surrounding missiles on the loose greatly intensified once the Cold War ended and governments realized they no longer had assurance they could control how these weapons would be used.

Prior to that flight, efforts to secure missiles were irregular and varied from government to government. For example, West Germany significantly improved airport security in the early 1970s after receiving threats that the terrorist Red Army Faction group would use a MANPADS to blow up a commercial Lufthansa airplane. Separately, the United States set up a study to understand the MANPADS threat against Americans. The government was interested in how MANPADS could be used in terrorist attacks. Such an attack would be less grave than a nuclear or biological attack. But it could still impact large numbers of people. Despite these efforts, missiles continued to spread readily through the gray and black markets.

BUYBACK PROGRAMS

In response to the threat of missiles being placed in enemy hands, the United States and other countries tried several tactics to control their spread. One of the methods was called a buyback program. A buyback program offers arms owners money or other compensation in exchange for their weapons.

Some missile buyback programs have had some success. In the weapons-in-exchange-for-development plan, the United States tried to trade farm and medical supplies with the Afghanis in return for Stinger missiles. Because Afghanistan was still in the middle of brutal conflict, the value of the weapons far surpassed the value of other goods. The program failed.

The missiles-for-other-weapons program, in which the United States traded machine guns and

Soviet Missiles Ignite Rwandan Genocide

In 1994, tension ran deep between the Hutu majority and the Tutsi minority of Rwanda. Though President Habyarimana negotiated for peace to end civil war with the Tutsi insurgent group, the Rwandan Patriotic Front, extremist Hutus continued to spew hatred and incite genocide on the radio.

SA-7 missiles sold from the Soviets to Uganda were used to attack the president's jet, igniting a brutal and swift genocide. Approximately 800,000 Tutsis were killed within 100 days. The perpetrators of the missile attack were never found.

Brazilian police confiscated thousands of arms
in an effort to stop illegal weapons imports in July 2002.

other firearms for missiles, took a slightly different
approach but also failed. Machine guns could
not compete with the "silver bullets," or missiles,
that had achieved such a high status among the
mujahideen.

Finally, governments implemented missiles-
for-cash programs. This tended to work better than
similar firearms-for-cash programs. These programs
sometimes worked because missiles were less

widespread and less numerous than firearms. In one successful missiles-for-cash program in 2003, the United States bought 41 SA-7 missiles from Hussein Aideed, a Somali warlord. Aideed had purchased the weapons with the intent to attack Ethiopia and protect Eritrean rebels. By the time the United States approached him, he had signed a peace truce with Ethiopia. The missiles were no longer useful to him.

Why Buy Back?

In order for buyback programs to work, psychological, social, and cultural factors must be considered. Though the United States solicited help from half a dozen countries and spent an estimated $65 million trying to buy back missiles from Afghanistan in the 1990s, hundreds remained missing. The Afghanis were unwilling to sell their arms. Afghan commander Abdul Hag summed up the dilemma from an Afghani's perspective: "You lose prestige if you get rid of them for money. The missiles are an enormous status symbol."[1] Owners of missiles would not be willing to sell missiles for cash if they felt it would hurt their ability to negotiate and show power.

Critics have also pointed out the moral problem of the "missiles-for-other-weapons" approach. In this program, the purchasing government buys missiles in exchange for weapons to protect the lives of its own citizens or allies. Though their allies may be safer, nations with new weapons in the hands of terrorists often use the tools against their own people.

COMPLICATIONS WITH BUYBACK PROGRAMS

Buyback programs are just one method

Missiles in Iraq

Between 1980 and 1988, $61 billion worth of weapons were sold to Iraq. By 1990, Iraq owned the fourth-largest military in the world. In 1994, following the Gulf War, the General Accounting Office (an investigative office of the US Congress) examined how the US Army had accounted for more than 6,000 Stinger missiles that had been sent to Iraq during the war. Investigators were disturbed to find Stingers abandoned on the side of the road. The army claimed it had 6,373 Stingers, but it was not able to provide serial numbers to track them, and 40 were never returned.

After the second Iraq War in 2003, 1 million tons (910,000 tonnes) of weaponry were left in the region. Yet no one was guarding the arms. Iraqi civilians walked away with armloads of weapons. The United States began destroying weapons to control their spread. As many as 100 tons (91 tonnes) per day in October 2003 were destroyed.

New York Times correspondent Raymond Bonner described the situation in Bagdad:

"Not a soldier or a guard was to be seen . . . missiles are everywhere . . . there is a 30-foot missile with Russian markings, still on its trolley. . . . Two Exocet missiles . . . lie on the ground several hundred yards away. They seem to have been rendered largely useless by the bombing, but parts may be of some value."[2]

governments use to try to curb the proliferation of missiles and small arms. Efforts have been made to catch and convict illicit small arms traders with some positive results. Others have proposed technological changes, such as installing codes in missiles to regulate their use. With all of these efforts, control of missile trade has been met with mixed results.

A somewhat successful buyback program occurred in Iraq. In May 2004, the United States wanted to reduce the number of weapons on the loose following the fall of Iraq's government. The United States tried to buy back weapons for cash. An AK-47 could be sold to the US government for $125. The amount of weapons on the streets or in stockpiles was reduced from 600,000 tons (544,311 tonnes) to 250,000 tons (226,796 tonnes). But still, many weapons were unaccounted for.

Investigations

There has been a series of investigations into illegal Stinger trades. One investigation determined that Kevin Gilday was using front companies abroad and fake end-user certificates among other faulty documentation to sell to the Irish Republican Army and other dangerous groups. In another investigation, a father-and-son team attempted to arm Iranians. The son called a leading American arms manufacturing company and offered a $100,000 bribe in exchange for necessary brokering paperwork. The father and son were quickly arrested. In another incident, two Irishmen in a south Florida bar boasted that they wanted to kill British troops in Northern Ireland with a sniper rifle. A fellow bar patron called the FBI, a sale was staged, and the men were arrested.

Missile Codes

A different approach to controlling the spread and misuse of missiles is more technological. Controlled enablers would work similarly to anti-theft devices on car radios. In order to operate an enabled missile, a user would have to enter the proper code. Without the code, the missile would malfunction and not be able to locate its target. Proponents of this approach believe this would result in fewer stolen missiles and reduce the black market demand. In turn, this would reduce the terrorist threat against commercial airlines.

The control enabler technology has been available since the 1980s. It would cost $1 million to design but still has not been put into effect. This may be partly due to costs associated with installing enablers.

Part of the problem with buyback programs is that people can easily exploit them. For example, some Iraqis sold weapons to the US government only to turn around and buy better ones on the black market. Others purchased weapons inexpensively on the black market and sold them to the US government to turn a profit.

No method of arms control can completely eliminate the illicit spread of arms or the abuse of arms throughout the world. Yet efforts such as buyback programs, sting operations, and international agreement on arms regulation may provide more hope for the future of this issue.

Approximately 2,500 illicit firearms were publicly destroyed in Nairobi, Kenya, in March 2010.

Protesters gathered in London to oppose arms trade in September 2009 while the Defence and Security Equipment International exhibition was held.

THE FUTURE
OF ARMS TRADE

On September 8, 2009, hundreds of protestors in London joined together against the opening of the Defence and Security Equipment International (DSEi), the world's largest arms fair. The protestors targeted DSEi's corporate investors by breaking windows and throwing paint bombs at banks. Members of the group DISARM DSEi believe these actions were justified. Member Sophie Williams said, "Any damage caused pales into insignificance in comparison with the destruction UK weapons have caused worldwide."[1] Masked and willing to fight, the protestors represent one extreme of the global arms debate.

Yet the current state of the arms trade has supporters and detractors on all sides of the issue. Some are horrified by the human rights injustices that occur because of the availability of weapons in unstable regions of the world. Many are terrified of becoming the victims of terrorist attacks. Others look to the future to ask how the people of the twenty-first century might begin to work out this global crisis—a crisis that has taken the lives of innocent people everywhere and become deeply entangled in our economic, social, and political reality.

"For too long, the world has been complacent about the devastating effect of the unregulated flow of arms. All countries participate in the conventional arms trade and share responsibility for the 'collateral damage' it produces—widespread death, injuries and human rights abuses. Finally, governments have agreed to negotiate legal controls on this deadly trade."[2]
—*Rebecca Peters, Director of International Action Network on Small Arms*

Most experts on arms trade believe that there is a need for international agreement to stop the unregulated spread of arms. An international policy would help prevent trade on the gray market where national loopholes are exploited. Experts expect sales of weapons on the black market would decrease, as a result. Some attempts to do this have been made through negotiations among multiple nations.

WASSENAAR ARRANGEMENT

One attempt to regulate arms trade came with the creation of the Wassenaar Arrangement (WA) in 1995. With 40 member states, the WA has established certain standards for export. It also has set controls for specific weapons that could cause significant damage, such as MANPADS. The WA is important because most major exporters are members, including the United States and Russia.

However, the WA is still limited. Participating countries agreed to operate according to certain standards, but there is nothing in the policy that monitors or enforces that compliance. One requirement of the agreement asserts that member states must inform all the other member states if they refuse to sell arms to a particular region or party.

Yet, there is no policy that prevents any of the other states from selling to the rejected region or party.

UN Programme of Action

Another step to regulate the spread of illicit arms was taken in the early years of the twenty-first century with the creation of the UN Programme of Action. With 189 participating countries, this program aimed to control black market arms sales. Many of the original plans for the program—expanding embargoes, improving weapons tracking, making illicit weapons possession a criminal offense, and destroying surpluses—were never set to action as hoped. However, during the 2008 biennial meeting, participants focused on making certain improvements. They discussed reducing illicit arms brokering, managing arms stocks better, and improving cooperation between different countries. Still, the program does not address the weapons that currently exist and can be easily traded illegally.

EU Code of Conduct

The EU Code of Conduct is a set of common guidelines and understandings for its members. In 2008, it was adopted as a common position among

all countries in the European Union (EU). The
legislative body adopted a common military list
of different equipment considered to be arms, a
common position on arms brokering, and shared
regulations for the export of torture devices. As
each country's individual law is forced to adapt to
the code, the regulation of arms is more consistent
across the EU.

However, one shortcoming of this policy is
that it only helps to control exports. There is no
inspection or monitoring of weapons after they
leave the country of origin. Some member countries
have complained that it is too easy to get around
the policy. They claim that other members, such
as Britain, have abused the policy and sold arms to
human rights violators.

The Arms Trade Treaty

The Arms Trade Treaty may be the most far-
reaching plan that has been put forth by policy
makers to date. The proposed treaty attempts to
bring all current legislation together under one
umbrella with everyone operating by the same shared
standards. This policy acknowledges the social and
economic factors that contribute to the varying effects

the arms trade has on different regions. The treaty would also be legally binding by international law.

In 2006, the UN General Assembly announced that the first resolution toward the Arms Trade Treaty had passed. Resolution 61/89 is intended to guide the establishment of the international policy. Protection of human rights is a guiding principle of the treaty. The Control Arms Campaign has come up with an additional 5 Golden Rules to address the impact of arms on human

Resolution 61/89 and the Campaign for the Arms Trade Treaty

In 2006, the UN General Assembly passed Resolution 61/89 with a vote of 153 against 1. The United States voted against the resolution. Twenty-four other countries abstained from voting, including major arms manufacturers such as Russia, India, Israel, and China.

The United States, however, voted in favor of the treaty in 2009 when the UN General Assembly voted to finalize the treaty by 2012. Zimbabwe voted against it. China and Russia abstained.

Three organizations have spearheaded the campaign for the Arms Trade Treaty: Oxfam, Amnesty International, and the International Action Network on Small Arms. Their efforts led to progress toward establishing an international arms policy. That policy includes the following principles detailed in Resolution 61/89:

Acknowledging the right of all States to manufacture, import, export, transfer and retain conventional arms for self-defence and security needs, and in order to participate in peace support operations . . . .

Acknowledging the growing support across all regions for concluding a legally binding instrument negotiated on a non-discriminatory, transparent and multilateral basis, to establish common international standards for the import, export and transfer of conventional arms.[3]

Politicians gathered in Dublin, Ireland, in September 2008 to show their support for Amnesty International's new report on the arms trade.

rights violations, terrorism, economic instability, and violent crime.

In 2008, the UN General Assembly reported that it would conduct additional research to understand the best path forward in establishing the Arms Trade Treaty in a way that would deal with many complex issues. The General Assembly advised all UN members to operate with the highest exporting standards during the research and planning phase.

The move toward the international Arms Trade Treaty is a major step toward managing many of the arms issues. Yet several major arms manufacturers have not supported it. This lack of support might make it difficult to enforce the treaty and to ensure that it has a long-lasting, meaningful effect.

In 2009, the UN took another step toward making this treaty a reality. Members voted to finalize the treaty in July 2012.

THE FUTURE

Small arms have caused much of the death and social unrest in conflict areas over the past several decades. Stable countries have increasingly feared the threat of mass destruction and terrorism. As technology

The 5 Golden Rules

The Control Arms Campaign has proposed 5 Golden Rules to guide the creation of the Arms Trade Treaty. These rules state that:

"States shall not authorise international transfers of conventional arms or ammunition where they will:

(i) be used or are likely to be used for gross violations of international human rights law or serious violations of international humanitarian law.

(ii) have an impact that would clearly undermine sustainable development or involve corrupt practices;

(iii) provoke or exacerbate armed conflict in violation of their obligations under the UN Charter and existing treaties.

(iv) contribute to an existing pattern of violent crime.

(v) risk being diverted for one of the above outcomes or for acts of terrorism."[4]

develops, there has been a move toward new forms of weaponry, including biochemical. All of these factors have shown the importance of international standards for arms trade.

Some economists and other strategists have looked toward other solutions for managing the arms trade. These solutions have less to do with law enforcement and legislation and more to do with sustainability. They look for opportunities to transform the small arms industry so that arms manufacturers would replace production of arms technologies with civil technologies that serve a purpose for growth and development. These supporters believe that the best path forward will be the development of tools aimed to improve environmental sustainability and help the world prepare for climate changes.

It is possible that changing social, economic, and environmental conditions could open the door to new opportunities for industry and development. These changes could begin to alter, and possibly replace, the arms trade.

Amnesty International erected mock gravestones in London in 2003 to draw attention to arms trade: One person is killed every minute by arms.

TIMELINE

600–900 CE	1944	1970s –1980s
Gunpowder is invented.	Soviet soldier Mikhail Kalashnikov develops the AK-47.	Libyan dictator Mu'ammar al-Gadhafi spends millions equipping terrorist groups with arms.

1987	1989	1990 –1991
Saudi Arabia, the United States, and other countries send $630 million worth of arms to Afghanistan.	The Berlin Wall falls and opens up paths for more weapons trade.	Iraq invades Kuwait and the United States leads liberation.

1978	1979	1982–1986
Air Rhodesia's flight 825 crashes as a result of the first missile attack on civilians by terrorists.	Idi Amin is overthrown after killing 200,000 Ugandans during his reign of terror.	President Ronald Reagan battles Congress in an attempt to export missiles to Saudi Arabia.

1991	1992–1995	1994
Afghanistan defeats the Soviet Union; the Cold War ends.	The Bosnian War occurs.	Rwandan President Habyarimana is killed by a missile attack, igniting the Rwandan genocide.

TIMELINE

1996	1997–2003	2000
A Paris-bound flight from New York crashes. The media suggests it is a missile attack, and legislators respond quickly with new policies.	Reign of Liberian dictator Charles Taylor, a key player in the human rights abuse of the diamond trade.	Major arms broker Leonid Minin is arrested in Italy but released in 2002 because he has not violated Italian national law.

2003–present	2003	2006
The United States and the United Kingdom lead an invasion of Iraq, suspecting the government holds weapons of mass destruction. The Iraq War begins.	The US military overthrows Saddam Hussein's forces in April. Weapons arsenals are left unguarded.	The United Nations General Assembly votes to begin work on the internationally binding Arms Trade Treaty.

2001

On September 11, al-Qaeda terrorists launch attacks on the United States.

2001

The largest British arms exhibition is held on September 16.

2008

Viktor Bout is arrested in a sting operation when he attempts to sell weapons to Colombian rebels.

2009

The United Nations General Assembly votes to pursue and finalize the Arms Trade Treaty by July 2012.

2010

Bout is extradited to the United States on November 16.

ESSENTIAL FACTS

AT ISSUE

❖ The most deadly and most common of all firearms are small arms or light weapons. There are at least 550 million known firearms around the world today.

❖ The United States is the largest exporter of weapons in the world, exporting approximately 30 percent of all arms. Other major exporters include Russia, Germany, France, and Britain. China, India, United Arab Emirates, Greece, and South Korea are the top importers of weapons.

❖ Small arms trade has become a large issue partly because of its negative effect on unstable nations. Some governments spend money on weaponry while neglecting large socioeconomic issues such as poverty, hunger, and health care.

❖ The lack of international law on arms trade has allowed arms brokers to exploit the arms trade system. Brokers can find loopholes in national laws, allowing them to conduct illicit sales to the most conflict-ridden regions of the world.

❖ Most experts on arms trade agree there is a need for international agreement to stop the unregulated spread of arms to conflict regions. Attempts to control arms trade have been made through buyback programs, controlled enablers, and legislation. Yet these attempts have been met with mixed success.

CRITICAL DATES

1944
The AK-47 was developed by Soviet soldier Mikhail Kalashnikov. It has become an iconic symbol of small arms trade and the most plentiful and widely used weapon in the world.

1991
Afghanistan defeated the Soviet Union, corresponding to the end of the Cold War. Alliances established during the Cold War led to the development of many of the pathways that continue to mark the modern-day arms trade.

1996

A Paris-bound flight from New York crashed. Media suggested it was a missile attack, and legislators scrambled to create policies to curb missile proliferation.

2006

The United Nations General Assembly voted to begin work on the internationally binding Arms Trade Treaty. The treaty may be the most far-reaching plan that has been put forth by policy makers. It attempts to bring all the current legislation together under one umbrella with everyone operating by the same shared standards. It would also be legally binding by international law. The United Nations will vote to pursue and finalize the treaty by July 2012.

QUOTES

"Small arms almost always outlast the political relationships that existed between the original supplier and recipient, and one needs look no farther than the anti-US activities of Osama bin Laden and his network of the former Afghan freedom fighters to see how covert arms sales can come back to haunt the supplier nations."
—*William Hartung, World Policy Institute*

"For too long, the world has been complacent about the devastating effect of the unregulated flow of arms. All countries participate in the conventional arms trade and share responsibility for the 'collateral damage' it produces—widespread death, injuries and human rights abuses. Finally, governments have agreed to negotiate legal controls on this deadly trade." —*Rebecca Peters, Director of International Action Network on Small Arms*

GLOSSARY

arsenal
> A collection or supply of weapons or munitions.

black market
> Trading that is done illegally.

compliance
> Cooperation or obedience with laws or regulations.

corrupt
> Guilty of dishonest practices such as bribery; lacking integrity; crooked.

disclosure
> The act or process of revealing or uncovering information.

embargo
> A restraint or prohibition on trade.

end user
> The ultimate user of a finished product.

extradite
> To give up an alleged criminal to be tried by another nation or authority.

gray market
> A description of trading that is not explicitly illegal but occurs undercover.

guerilla
> A member of an irregular military unit operating in small bands that specialize in harassing and undermining the enemy, as in a surprise raid.

icon
> An important and enduring symbol.

insurgent
> A member of a section of a political party who revolts against the methods or policies of the party.

mercenaries
> Private armies that are paid for by governments.

pastoralist
> A person who bases a social and economic system on the raising and herding of livestock.

precursor
> Something that precedes and points to something that follows.

proliferation
> A rapid increase in number or spread, often excessively.

protocol
> An agreement between states or authoritative parties.

surplus
> An amount or quantity of weapons greater than needed.

transit states
> Countries through which weapon shipments pass on their way to the recipient state.

ADDITIONAL RESOURCES

SELECTED BIBLIOGRAPHY

Burrows, Gideon. *The No-Nonsense Guide to the Arms Trade.* Oxford, UK: New Internationalist Publications, 2002. Print.

Gilby, Nicholas. *The No-Nonsense Guide to the Arms Trade.* Oxford, UK: New Internationalist Publications, 2009. Print.

Saywell, Shelley. *Devil's Bargain.* Bishari Film Productions, 2008. DVD.

Small Arms Survey. *Small Arms Survey 2001: Profiling the Problem.* Oxford, UK: Oxford University Press, 2001. Print.

Small Arms Survey. *Small Arms Survey 2009: Shadows of War.* Cambridge, UK: Cambridge University Press, 2009. Print.

Stohl, Rachel, Matt Schroeder, and Dan Smith. *The Arms Trade: A Beginner's Guide.* Oxford, UK: Oneworld Publications, 2007. Print.

FURTHER READINGS

Bingley, Richard. *The Arms Trade.* Chicago, IL: Raintree, 2003. Print.

Gifford, Clive. *The Arms Trade (World Issues).* London, UK: Chrysalis Children's Books, 2004. Print.

Hibbert, Adam. *The Arms Trade (In the News).* London, UK: Franklin Watts, 2003. Print.

WEB LINKS

To learn more about arms trade, visit ABDO Publishing Company online at **www.abdopublishing.com**. Web sites about arms trade are featured on our Book Links page. These links are routinely monitored and updated to provide the most current information available.

For More Information

For more information on this subject, contact or visit the following organizations.

Campaign Against Arms Trade
1 Goodwin Street, Finsbury Park, London N4 3HQ
44-207-281-0297
www.caat.org.uk
Become more aware of global issues related to arms trade, such as human rights and economic security. The campaign aims to eventually abolish the international arms trade.

Coalition to Stop Gun Violence
www.csgv.org
Link to a number of ways to get involved in reducing gun-related violence.

Control Arms Campaign
c/o Amnesty International
1 Easton Street, London WC1X 0DW, UK
44-207-413-5500
www.controlarms.org
Find more information about global arms trade and the proposed Arms Trade Treaty at this site.

United States Campaign to Ban Landmines
6930 Carroll Avenue, Suite 240, Takoma Park, MD 20912
301-891-2138
www.icbl.org
Get involved in efforts to ban the use, production, and export of land mines.

Source Notes

Chapter 1. Born to Kill
1. *Devil's Bargain.* Dir. Shelley Saywell. Bishari Film Productions, 2008. DVD.
2. Ibid.
3. Ibid.

Chapter 2. From Bow and Arrow to AK-47
1. Rachel Stohl, Matt Schroeder, and Dan Smith. *The Arms Trade: A Beginner's Guide.* Oxford, UK: Oneworld Publications, 2007. Print. 22.
2. *Devil's Bargain.* Dir. Shelley Saywell. Bishari Film Productions, 2008. DVD.
3. Rachel Stohl, Matt Schroeder, and Dan Smith. *The Arms Trade: A Beginner's Guide.* Oxford, UK: Oneworld Publications, 2007. Print. 7.

Chapter 3. Weapons Changing Hands
1. William Hartung. "The New Business of War: Small Arms and the Proliferation of Conflict." *Ethics & International Affairs.* Questia Media America, Inc. 2001. Web. 30 Aug. 2010.

Chapter 4. The Role of the Law
None.

Chapter 5. Guns and Diamonds
1. Rachel Stohl, Matt Schroeder, and Dan Smith. *The Arms Trade: A Beginner's Guide.* Oxford, UK: Oneworld Publications, 2007. Print. vi.
2. *Devil's Bargain.* Dir. Shelley Saywell. Bishari Film Productions, 2008. DVD.
3. Gideon Burrows. *No-Nonsense Guide to the Arms Trade.* Oxford, UK: New International Publications, 2002. Print. 8.

Chapter 6. Small Arms, Big Problems

1. Small Arms Survey. *Small Arms Survey 2001: Profiling the Problem.* Oxford, UK: Oxford University Press, 2001. Print. 60.

2. Nicholas Gilby. *No-Nonsense Guide to the Arms Trade.* Oxford, UK: New Internationalist Publications, 2009. Print. 117.

Chapter 7. Man-Portable Missiles

1. Rachel Stohl, Matt Schroeder, and Dan Smith. *The Arms Trade: A Beginner's Guide.* Oxford, UK: Oneworld Publications, 2007. Print. 78.

2. Ibid. 74.

3. Ibid. 88.

4. Ibid.

5. Ibid. 78.

6. Ibid. 80.

7. Ibid. 112.

Chapter 8. Buying Back Control

1. Rachel Stohl, Matt Schroeder, and Dan Smith. *The Arms Trade: A Beginner's Guide.* Oxford, UK: Oneworld Publications, 2007. Print. 93.

2. Ibid. 116.

Chapter 9. The Future of Arms Trade

1. Disarm DSEi. "Corporate Investors Attacked at Anti Arms Trade Action." *dsei.org.* n.d. Web. 8 Sept. 2009.

2. International Action Network on Small Arms. "World Unites to Tackle Global Arms Trade." *iansa.org.* IANSA, n.d. Web. 27 Jul. 2010.

3. United Nations General Assembly. "Towards an arms trade treaty: establishing common international standards for the import, export and transfer of conventional arms." *disarmament. un.org.* United Nations, 17 Aug. 2007. Web. 2 Sept. 2010.

4. Control Arms. "Golden Rules for an Arms Trade Treaty." *Controlarms.org.* Control Arms, n.d. Web. 5 Dec. 2009.

INDEX

INDEX CONTINUED

ABOUT THE AUTHOR

Ashley Rae Harris is a freelance writer who lives and works in Chicago, Illinois. She has an MA from the University of Chicago where she focused her research on youth culture and identity. She has written several books on the topic of adolescent self-esteem, a celebrity biography, and several articles for various magazines and online publications, including *Venuszine* and *Time Out Chicago*.

PHOTO CREDITS

AP Images, cover, 3, 23, 24, 33; Farah Abdi Warsameh, File/AP Images, 6; Mohamed Sheikh Nor/AP Images, 13; Jens Meyer, File/AP Images, 14, 96 (top); Charles Dharapak/AP Images, 17; Sipa/AP Images, 21, 96 (bottom); Joe Gaal/AP Images, 26; Michael Straveto/AP Images, 31; Apichart Weerawong/AP Images, 34, 99 (bottom); Swoan Parker/AP Images, 40; Mark J. Terrill/AP Images, 45; David Guttenfelder/AP Images, 46, 98; Red Line Editorial, Inc., 50, 53; Kristy Wigglesworth/AP Images, 55, 99 (top); Saleh Rifai/AP Images, 56; Musadeq Sadeq/AP Images, 61; Burhan Ozbilici/AP Images, 65; Darron Cummings, Files/AP Images, 66; David Stewart Smith/AP Images, 70; Ben Curtis/AP Images, 75; Emilio Morenatti/AP Images, 76, 97; Renzo Gostoli/AP Images, 80; Khalil Senosi/AP Images, 85; Sang Tan/AP Images, 86; Niall Carson, PA Wire/AP Images, 92; Alastair Grant/AP Images, 95